www.united-pc.eu

T J DENCH

A FORCE 4 CHANGE

HYPNOSIS

A detailed look into how Hypnosis can help make lasting lifestyle changes

A FORCE 4 CHANGE

A Force 4

Change

Hypnosis

Contents

Introduction

Introduction

I was first introduced to Hypnosis when I was a child aged about ten.

I bought a book in a car boot sale, at my local youth club. It was called the magic eye. I remember buying it thinking it would be a fantasy story, or even a horror.

I also remember the feeling of excitement when I realized that it was a book revealing the secrets of Hypnosis.

I read the book from cover to cover. And I was amazed. I practiced and practiced with a friend from school. I feel bad now because I can't remember his name now. I lost the book as I got older. I guess I became a teenager and although my interest was still there, it got pushed aside as other events unfolded, and other things took priority.

But I never lost my interest.

Now 30 years on I've worked as a mechanic, enjoyed a 13-year career in the army where I met, and fought besides some great guys and girls. I've had my own Pub and met some amazing people there. I've also worked in the UK's Prison system, as a contractor escort and a prison officer. So, it's fair to say I've worked and served with the best and the worst of people.

During all this I never lost my passion for hypnosis.

Most people see the stage hypnotist, and think it is only weak-minded people who must get hypnotized. They think this because they act like idiots. There is a reason they do that which will be explained in this book. And a good hypnotist, even a stage hypnotist wouldn't make you look like an idiot. You can be respectful while still having fun.

I'm writing this Book to spread the word of this amazing gift. And that's exactly what it is, it's a gift.

By the end of this book, I hope you will see that whatever you can focus your mind on, it can achieve.

The Truth is anyone can be Hypnotized, and anyone can be the Hypnotist. Some are easier than others. A study showed that 20% of people are great hypnotic subjects 20% are difficult but most of us fall in the middle.

A FORCE 4 CHANGE

There are a number of stages that make up the hypnotic cycle.

These are:

Pre-Talk

Induction

Deepeners

Suggestion

Emergence

Master each section and you will be an unstoppable hypnotist.

Why the sub title Force 4 Change?

Well I chose Force 4 Change because I believe that to make lasting change we need to focus on 4 areas.
The 4 areas I've identified in this book, I believe are all linked. And if we neglect even one of them, then it will have a knock-on effect on the other.
I believe we need to take back control of all these areas to lead the life we deserve. Of course, Hypnosis isn't the only avenue which we can explore to achieve this. But for the purposes of this book that's where I'm focussing my attention. By using hypnosis to focus on

these areas you will notice a major
change. Lasting change.

These areas are:

Mental health.
Being free from anxiety and stress. Being
comfortable in our own self being

Diet.
Being in control of your diet. Eating
when you want, and eating well while
still losing weight. This is something we
all want and can do. We just need to do
it right.

Physical health.
Having the motivation to exercise and the
mindset to make small changes to be a
fitter version of our selves. Helping us
feel better

Spiritual health.
Not necessarily religious. But having
something to focus and calm the mind.

Working on these 4 areas in life, will
give you a better quality of life. Where
you are in control of your own destiny.
I'll cover all of these areas in this
book.
I will even throw in some EFT (Emotional
Freedom Technique)

Chapter One

A BREIF HISTORY

If you're looking to get good at Hypnosis it's a good idea to learn a bit about where it came from and how it evolved.

This would be a huge book if I went in depth on every key figure and how they influenced hypnosis and all the different techniques and how they differ. For this reason, here is I brief history.

The earliest users of hypnosis I'd say were shaman and witch Dr's. inducing trance for ceremony, ritual and healing.

Key figures which I'm concentrating on in the western world would be Franz Mesmer, James braid, Emile Coue, Milton Ericson and Dave Elman. There are many more but I'll keep it to these.

If you do your own research, it will help you to put things in to your own words. This will help you gain your own perspective, for when you educate your clients.

Some won't be interested, but others will ask and try and test you.

And the more you seem to be the subject matter expert, the more confidence your clients will have in you. And there for the easier the whole process becomes.

Franz Anton Mesmer (1734-1815)

Franz Mesmer was an Austrian physician commonly known by many as one of the Fathers of Hypnosis. The word "mesmerism" is derived from his name. After graduating from a famous school in Vienna he became interested in the use of magnets over the body for healing. His theory of "animal magnetism" which says that blockages in the flow of magnetic forces in the body causes diseases. This belief if echoed in other holistic therapies such as Emotional freedom techniques and thought field therapy or even acupuncture.

Mesmer is known for his belief that a kind of magnetic energy surround us, and that he could store his animal magnetism in baths of iron filings which he said could be transferred to his patients with rods and by flamboyant "mesmeric passes". He claimed that through this his patients were cured of their illnesses.

His lengthy ritualistic procedure could

last for hours, and it is said that the patient's boredom was what actually made them go into a trance!

A royal commission was appointed to investigate his findings. They could find no evidence to support his theories of animal magnetism. They concluded, Mesmer must be an 'impostor'. Mesmer stopped his practice until his death in 1815.

James Braid (1795-1860)

James Braid was a Scottish eye doctor practicing in Manchester, England. We owe the term hypnotism to him. He developed his interest in mesmerism by chance while late for an appointment with a patient. When he walked into the waiting room he found his patient staring into an old lamp, with his eyes glazed. Fascinated, he started giving the patient some commands and found that the patient complied, such as closing his eyes and going to sleep. It was then that he discovered that an important component in putting a person into a trance is to have them fixate on something. Braid published a book, proposing that the phenomenon be called "hypnotism".

Emile Coue` (1857-1926)

Coue pioneered the use of autosuggestion. He is famous for the phrase (loosely translated) "Every day, in every way, I'm getting better and better" His technique focused on positive affirmation and believed that he did not heal people himself, instead, only facilitated their own self-healing. He believed "there is no such thing as hypnosis, only self-hypnosis". One of his most famous ideas was that imagination is more powerful than the will.

A technique he developed for self-hypnosis or auto suggestion was with a piece of string.

Tie 20-30 knots evenly spaced in a length of string.

Before you lay down to bed and as soon as you wake up hold the tip of the string in one hand. Focus your attention on the string. Now at the top of the string with the other hand use your index finger and thumb to lightly pinch the string.

Pinch the string light enough for it to slip through your finger and thumb as you slowly run them down the string.

As you reach each knot say the phrase "Every day, in every way, I'm getting

better and better" using this technique
brought some amazing results.

Milton H. Erickson, MD (1901-1980)

Milton Erikson was an American
psychiatrist and is called by many the
"Father of Modern Hypnotherapy" because
of his contributions to the acceptance of
the practice. He is said to be a gifted
observer, able to easily build rapport
with his clients. His therapeutic tools
included metaphors and stories, memorable
imagery, surprise and humor and a
deceptive conversational style. His
practice is known as "Ericksonian
Hypnosis". He has influenced modern
schools of hypnosis and Neuro Linguistic
programing.

Dave Elman (1900-1967)

Dave Elman was a modern pioneer of the
medical use of hypnosis. In fact, he
contributed greatly to the acceptance of
hypnosis by the medical community. He
trained a lot of physicians, dentists and
psychiatrists on how to use hypnotism.
These medical practitioners paved the way
towards the acceptance of hypnosis and
hypnotherapy as a valid treatment that

could work hand-in-hand with conventional medical treatments.

His inductions and techniques are taught, used and practiced by many professional hypnotists today.

Chapter Two

MYTHS AND FREQUENTLY ASKED QUESTIONS

Thanks to the TV, film and popular fiction there are many myths associated with Hypnosis.

As part of your pre-talk you will need to dispel these myths and educate the subject to help them feel comfortable.

All the while building repour. The client will have to trust you completely, and want to go into hypnosis.

If the client doesn't trust you they won't want you poking around their mind so you'll be fighting a losing battle.

Again, if they don't like you they won't want to work with you.

First let's deal with the myths.

These Myths are listed below. I've written them in the form of the questions you might get asked.

- Can I get stuck in hypnosis?

- Can I be made to do things against my will?

- Will I be made to tell my deepest darkest secrets?

- If this works does it mean I'm week willed or simple minded.

The above are the most common misconceptions associated with Hypnosis that people seem to have. you will need to ease people's fears and educate them about these in order to increase your chances to hypnotize them.

With practice you can work these into a pre-talk naturally.

Here are some more Frequently asked questions

- Can anyone be Hypnotized?

- Is there an ideal Hypnotic subject?

- Will I be unconscious?

- What will I need to do?

- Are there any side effects?

- What does it feel like?

- What if I'm seeing a Dr and taking medication?

- How long will each session last?

- Can hypnosis be dangerous?

- How will I know that I'm hypnotized?

- How many sessions will I need?

- And will the effects ware off if I stop coming?

Let's Debunk The Myths

Can I get stuck in hypnosis?

No, you cannot get stuck in Hypnosis. Hypnosis is a natural state of mind that everybody slips in and out of every day.

Ever found yourself staring out of a window seemingly fixated on something and your mind wandering thinking about

something else. Or when you're out
driving and pull up at your destination
and can't remember how you got there,
must have been on autopilot. Both
examples of light hypnotic states.

If for any reason during a hypnosis
session the Hypnotist stops, leaves or
even drops dead, then one of two things
might happen. You will be so relaxed that
you will fall asleep and awaken
naturally, or you will become aware that
something is not right, and then just
open your eyes when you are ready.

I know some hypnotists have experimented
with the idea of proving this myth and
not disproving the myth. By given a
certain suggestion not allowing the
subject to come out of hypnosis.

And they had a certain level of success.
The suggestion was something like this.

"as you drift further into hypnosis you
will feel better and better. The deeper
into hypnosis you go the better you will
feel. And if you try to open your eyes at
anytime you will go even further into
hypnosis feeling even better.

The more you try to wake out of hypnosis
the deeper you go and the better you
feel. It feels so good to just drift
deeper and deeper."

Now this did work. The subject finds that if they tried to open their eyes they went deeper more relaxed. Making it hard to wake up from hypnosis. And its reinforced with the good feeling getting better and better. But in the end, they did snap out of it.

I suppose that the subconscious, while looking after the subject, realized they had to come around to survive.

Can I be made to do things against my will?

No, you can't be made to do anything that is against your will or moral judgment. You will have to be willing to go into hypnosis for it to work.

And in the same way you will have to be open to the suggestion for it to be able to work.

If a suggestion is made that is against your moral judgement then you will just reject it. You are always in control.

You might be thinking about the people on stage of a hypnosis show. well in this situation the volunteers expect to do those things and by agreeing to take part in the show, have agreed to do those things. But if the hypnotist breaks their

trust and asks them to give them all their money the subject will wake up and say no.

Will I be made to tell my deepest darkest secrets?

No, you can't be made to say anything that you really don't want to say.

For example, if the Hypnotist asked you to reveal your deepest secret or the pin number to your bank card you will reject the suggestion.

like I've stated previously you have to be willing for a suggestion to work.

Does it mean I'm weak willed or simple minded?

No, actually the opposite is true.

It's been proven that the more intelligent you are, the easier it is to be hypnotized. Partly due to having to multi task and stay focused.

During the hypnotic process you will need to concentrate, relax, focus and visualize as well as follow simple instructions.

it can be difficult to hypnotize a person with a mental disorder that affects attention and concentration, but it's not impossible.

FREQUENTLY ASKED QUESTIONS

Can anyone be Hypnotized?

Anybody that wants to be hypnotized can be but the reverse is also true

If somebody really doesn't want to be hypnotized, then they never will be.

The exception is that anyone with a mental disorder that effects concentration will find it difficult to focus enough to get hypnotized.

Is there an ideal Hypnotic subject?

The best hypnotic subject is:

- Someone who really wants to be hypnotized

- A good Visualizer

- Someone willing to cooperate fully with the therapist rather than sit back and let it all go over their head.

- Someone intelligent enough to understand the explanations and play a full part in the proceedings.

Will I be unconscious?

No, hypnosis is a pure state of focus and not a state of eyelids.

A side effect of hypnosis is relaxation, this is what you see when viewing someone under hypnosis.

You are wide awake and aware of everything going on and everything that is being said.

What will I need to do?

All that is necessary for you to do, is to comply with the hypnotist.

A good hypnotist will discuss what will be happening before the session, so that there are no surprises. So, if it's

necessary to speak, you will be told before the session that you will be asked to speak while still hypnotized. They will explain that although you will be hypnotized, it will not be possible for you to give away any secrets or personal information that you do not want to tell.

Are there any side effects?

The only side effect of hypnosis is relaxation. There are a lot of stories out there of hypnosis going wrong with lasting after effects.

Once you get rid of the nonsense you get to the more plausible effects that could have happened. I will try to explain them here.

I've heard of people coming out of stage hypnosis still feeling the effects.

There have been cases where the stage hypnotist hasn't taken away the suggestions after the show and left the volunteers with unwanted effects.

Stage hypnotists use a very light level of hypnosis with some very funny and amazing results. And because during the show the subjects are in and out of hypnosis, by the end of the show they are actually in quite deep. This will be explained later.

If the subjects are not awakened properly, they can suffer from something called the hypnotic hangover. This is an extremely drowsy feeling sometimes accompanied by a head ache.

And if the suggestions aren't taken away it doesn't mean you are left with them forever. The effects will normally fade over the course of the day or overnight after a good night's sleep.

If this doesn't work then it's a trip to a hypnotist to remove the suggestions.

Another unwanted effect can come from the hypnotist unintentionally putting suggestions in during a session.

I know a hypnotist with the worst potty mouth. Every other word is a swear word. This can be quite irresponsible. The reason...I heard of a man who used to say the word shit all the time. He'd say it all day without even realizing he was doing it. One day he suffered from a bout of diarrhea. But it didn't go away.

It went on for a few days so the man went to see a Dr and gave a sample.

The Dr couldn't find anything wrong.

The diarrhea carried on. Test after test they found nothing. Until a friend of the man went to a hypnotherapist and he tagged along.

It wasn't long before the man had to use the toilet and the situation was mentioned to the hypnotist.

The therapist noted that the man had said shit a few times in a short period.

He questioned the man who didn't realize and apologized. The man's friend then said you do say that word a lot.

The hypnotist explained how auto suggestion works and how he had a theory that the man unwillingly gave himself the suggestion to shit.

And that if this was the case he could help him and end his suffering possibly in one session.

The man agreed. Well he had nothing to lose.

At the guys amazement it worked.

So, as you can see if this is true, you can imagine the damage if the man had a hypnotherapist swearing saying all sorts of unmentionable words.

Could make a very funny stage show!

What does Hypnosis feel like?

Hypnosis is a beautiful relaxing experience that is unique to the individual.

If you close your eyes and breathe deeply and relax every muscle. Then you get a good idea. It's like a daydream state, but your fully aware of your surroundings.

Most people just feel very relaxed.

Some people feel like they are floating

Others feel like they are sinking into the chair or bed they are on.

What if I'm seeing a Dr and Taking medication?

The hypnotist is not necessarily a medical Dr, so cannot diagnose illness or prescribe any or take you off any drugs.

If you are on any medication for a mental condition then you must speak to a Dr before seeking Hypnotherapy and if you feel after the therapy that you don't need the medication then only a Dr can take you off them.

28

How long will a session last?

Well this depends on what the therapy is for and the therapist.

A typical hypnotherapy session can be anything from 20 minutes to a couple of hours.

Most are between 40 minutes to an hour for most fears' phobias or stress and anxiety.

If a session requires regression to a memory then it will last longer as you will be dictating while the therapist takes notes and decides where the session will need to go to best aid the therapy.

The same for future progression and life between life therapy.

A good therapist will let the client dictate the sessions length. Well its them helping themselves really you are just the guide.

Is Hypnosis Dangerous?

No, the only danger is you falling over, or off the chair because you get so relaxed.

As long as you have a good reputable hypnotherapist, who follows good safe working practices you will be safe.

Remember you can't be made to do anything you don't want to do, so in this way you will not except any suggestion that's going to harm you.

How will I know if I'm hypnotized?

Most people who get hypnotized for the first time are surprised to find how normal it feels. And do sometimes question whether they were hypnotized at all.

In this case it is down to the therapist/hypnotist to conduct tests.

The tests are not for the hypnotists benefit but for the subject.

The Hypnotist can see that the subject is in hypnosis by the flushing of the face, the shallowing of breathing and the flicker of the eyes as well as many other telltale signs an experienced hypnotist would pick up.

These tests could be the eye lock test. Arm lock test. Hand stick test. And many others.

Testing can help a novice hypnotist gain confidence in his own ability in early stages of his career but mainly are to allow the client to know that something is happening and they now, can start to make positive changes.

How many sessions will I need?

This depends. I've had success with clients in one session for stress, anxiety, confidence and phobias. I've also had clients that took 3 sessions to make the same changes.

Others need more it depends on how ready you are to make the changes that need to happen for you to become the person you want to be.

Will the effects ware off if I stop coming?

This is also dependent on how ready you are to make the changes needed.

Unlike the suggestions given in a stage hypnosis show. The suggestions given in a therapy environment are given because they are needed to help change your life to become the person you want to be, to live the life you want to live. So, the suggestions are accepted by your subconscious mind and the changes are made.

Whereas the suggestions made in a show
are for entertainment purposes where you
haven't built up that same level of trust
with the hypnotist. And if not taken away
will wear off over time. Your
subconscious will recognize that they are
only entertainment and not there to help
you. If it's no benefit to you, why make
it permanent.

It will also depend on your therapist and
the repour you have with them. If you
have a good therapist and have built up
trust and repour then the suggestions
will be embedded far better than if you
didn't quite trust the hypnotist.

Chapter Three

PRE-TALK

Now the Pre-Talk, this is the most important part of the Hypnotic cycle. The point is to give the subject an expectation of what's going to happen, and ease their fears.

It not only builds trust and repour but dispels any incorrect pre-conceptions and educates the subject about what they will be experiencing.

You can't Hypnotize someone without a pre-talk, no matter what you read or see on tv. Most of the work is done here.

The better the Pre-talk the better your success rate will be as a hypnotist.

Remember the Pre-Talk should make the subject comfortable give them confidence in your ability and build repour.

Depending on the situation depends on your pretalk

If you go to a stage hypnotist, the pre-talk will seem like the hypnotist is just talking while setting up, filling in on the quiet parts of the show. but again, it's the most important part. The Hypnotist will Throw some jokes in and try and get the crowd to like him, while keeping an air of mystery.

In the Street you may see that the hypnotist may have a sign or a T-shirt saying in big letters. PROFFESIONAL HYPNOTIST. ASK ME TO HYPNOTISE YOU AND FEEL AMAZING.

Now if someone comes to you and says do me, then they want to experience something, so your half way there.

It's your job then to make sure they do. But there still will be some sort of talk to comfort and put them at ease.

Here's an example of how I do mine.

Example

"Have you ever experienced Hypnosis before?"

Here you will get a yes or no. a Yes answer will make the whole process easier but here we will assume a No answer. But if I wasn't the hypnotist that saw him/her before I would pretty much still go through my pretalk.

"That's fine let me tell you a bit about Hypnosis."

Here is where we educate people about what hypnosis is and isn't.

"Hypnosis is a natural state that we all pop in and out of constantly through our lives.

Have you ever had a moment where you can't think of a person's name? A name you know really well but it's on the tip of your tongue, you just can't say it.

Or staring out a window completely fixated on a point but mind seemingly focused on something else, mind wondering or day dreaming.

or have you been walking or driving somewhere, arrived at the destination and can't remember how you got there, the journey's gone, completely forgotten.

these are all examples of a light hypnotic state.

The conscious mind is so relaxed the subconscious takes over.

Now to tell you what hypnosis isn't.

Some people think only the weak minded or simple minded can be hypnotized, Actually the opposite is true.

A FORCE 4 CHANGE

You have to relax, focus, concentrate,
visualize and follow simple instructions
all at the same time. So, the more
intelligent the person the better subject
they are.

You can't get stuck in hypnosis either.
If something was to happen, where you
find that I've stopped speaking or gone
away then one of two things will happen.
1, you'll wander what happened and open
your eyes or 2, you'll be so relaxed that
you fall asleep and wake up in your own
time.

You can't be made to do anything against
your will or moral judgment. when in
Hypnosis you're not asleep you are
actually aware of everything happening
around you, and everything that's said.
so, if something is against your morals
then you will reject the suggestion.

Also, in the same way you can't be made
to tell your deepest secrets. You'll just
reject the suggestion.

I'd like to show you how to access this
state of mind! Where we can make some
positive changes. Are you happy to do
that now?"

Chop and change this to suit you, and
help it flow better for you.

Next is the **YES set** and **COMPLIANCE set.**
I'll cover these in the induction because
it just flows straight in to it.

A FORCE 4 CHANGE

Chapter Four

INDUCTION

Here I'm going to show you how to effortlessly guide someone in to hypnosis.

I say guide because you are just a guide. As Emil Coue said all Hypnosis is self-Hypnosis. So, if it's not successful remember it's probably not you. As long as you follow everything here then it's probably the subject just isn't ready.

To increase the chances for success there is a few more stages to the induction. These are:

- Yes set

- Compliance set

Now once you've given a good pre-talk. Most books will brush over it or take you straight on to the induction but as stated we will go into a yes set.

A yes set is a set of questions that get the subject in to an agreeable frame of mind, this will also increase your success rate. And as you might have guessed, it can be any question that you know the answer will be yes.

YES SET

Question "Now Are you comfortable?"

Answer "YES" if its anything other than a yes

Tell them "make yourself comfortable now. Ok?

Answer "yes"

Question "Are you happy to experience hypnosis and make some positive changes?"

Answer "YES" Who wouldn't want to make positive changes and if they didn't want to experience hypnosis they wouldn't be there.

Question "Are you happy to allow me to guide you through hypnosis now to make some positive changes now?"

Answer "YES" again this is telling them

it's going to happen now and if they

didn't want to go into hypnosis they
wouldn't be there.

COMPLIANCE SET

Now we have the Yes set done we move on
to a Compliance set.

again, a set of Instructions rather than
questions in which we would like to get a
positive action

Instruction 1 "Sit back in the chair"

adapt to the Situation if standing you
can ask them to move "Stand here"

Instruction 2 "Place both feet flat on
the floor and hands on your lap." or if
standing "Place both feet shoulder width
apart so your steady on your feet"

again, this is to get the desired
response.

Instruction 3 "look here and focus on
this spot for the duration until I say
otherwise"

if standing you can move them a couple times if sitting or lying you can get them to position their hands. anything to get compliance.

Now that the subjects been prepared the best we can, we are more likely to succeed.

You will find your own style but speak clearly, slow and with authority but also calming. You will see.

I've had people say I sound very sexy when I'm talking in my Hypnotic voice lol. You will find yours.

Induction eye fixation

Pick a spot or object for them to focus on.

Just above their eyeline is best. Or something silhouetted by a light. It helps make the eyes tiered and heavy.

"I want you to focus on this spot here. That's it, look at this spot, and stare at it until I say otherwise.

Take three deep breaths…1 that's it all the way in and all the way out…2…that's right and on the third just hold… now exhale completely releasing any tension you have in your body.

Focus your eyes on that spot there, as you focus your eyes on that spot notice your breathing shallow as you just breath just as deep that is comfortable.

And Anytime you hear me say the words deeper you'll sink deeper into hypnosis doubling your relaxation and focus.

That's right. Relaxing completely.

Take another deep breath in, and exhale completely. Relaxing your shoulders and arms.

I want you to notice now how heavy your eyes are feeling as you focus on that spot.

And your eye lids as they blink and become even heavier and heavier and heavier.

Notice now how the more you blink, the heavier they seem to feel, and the heavier they feel the more you want to blink. And that's fine let it happen.

Notice the focus change as they become so heavy you just want to close them now.

43

A FORCE 4 CHANGE

Close your eyes and relax, sinking deeper
relaxing every muscle, nerve and fiber
more than ever before.

Sinking Ten times Deeper, twenty times
Deeper, thirty times Deeper, forty times,
fifty times, sixty times Deeper, seventy,
eighty, ninety times, one hundred times
Deeper than ever before, more relaxed
more focused.

That's right. sinking, drifting,
draining.

Focusing only on my voice.

Now I'd like you to become aware of where
your **stood/sat** feel the **seat/ground**
beneath keeping you secure, safe as you
go deeper, that's right.

Perfectly safe perfectly fine as you go
deeper.

notice the sounds around you, people
talking, moving, everyday life carrying
on.

just allow those sounds to take you
deeper more relaxed more focused than
ever before. You're doing really well.

Focus now on those tiny little muscles
around your eyes. Feel them relaxing
completely, each tiny muscle around your
eyes relaxing so much that your eyelids

wont work.

Your eye lids are so heavy, relaxed so
much they won't open, and that relaxation
feels so good you don't want them to
open.

It feels so good to be so relaxed feel it
spreading through your face.

Feel that relaxation spread like a wave
down your body and out through your toes.
Relaxing every muscle nerve and fiber."

This is a very short but affective
hypnosis script and easy to remember you
can lengthen it or shorten it depending
on your subject. If your pre-talk is good
this is all you'll need but you may like
to tweak it. You can see there is a
deepener in the induction you can take it
out and use another method if you like.

I like this one and I'd probably add
another deepener at the end of it like a
hand drop or a visualization method. Il
explain more on deepeners later.

There are many different hypnotic
inductions out there a lot are based
around this style.

Induction 2 Progressive muscle Relaxation.

This one is a classic method used by the majority of hypnotherapists out there.

It can be long winded but effective you can normally get good results even if the pretalk is poor. It's been said you just bore them into trance just like Mesmer.

"Now lay back put your arms by your sides and breath just as deep as is comfortable for you.

Good

Now as you lay there relaxing focus on your breathing, breathing in calm and relaxation and exhaling tension. Good, all the way in, and all the way out. Relaxing more and more.

That's right.

Now close your eyes.

Focus now on your eyes, focus all your attention on every tiny muscle around your eyes.

I want you to relax them completely. More and more with every breath.

Relax all those tiny muscles now.

Notice as you relax them more, and more, that heavy relaxed feeling.

Good. Feel that heavy relaxed feeling, feel it as it goes to your cheeks, relaxing them completely, and now up to your forehead.

That's right, relaxing your forehead. And down to your jaw. Feel it relaxing all those tiny muscles now.

Relax your neck. And your shoulders. Heavy, loose and limp. Notice how good it feels to be so relaxed.

Good.

Relaxing more with every breath.

Now, relax your upper arms. Your fore arms and relax your wrists completely, relaxed.

Relax your hands and fingers completely.

Feel that tingling feeling in your fingers. That's right, as they relax.

Feel that relaxation going back up your arms now and in to your shoulder again relaxing them even more.

That's it. It feels so good.

Now, drifting down your chest relaxing as it goes down like a wave of relaxation in

to your abs. relaxing your hips and your
groin.

Relaxing your thighs. Notice how nice it
is. How good it feels.

Relax your calves and your shins,
relaxing your ankles and feet.

Relaxing every little toe as it drifts
down like a wave of relaxation.

Feel this wave relaxing every muscle
nerve fiber of your body from the top of
your head to the tips of your toes".

If you feel the need you can go back up
through the muscle groups but I'd go
straight into another deepener.

Chapter Five

DEEPENERS

A deepener is a method of taking a subject to a deeper level of Hypnosis.

The deeper you go the more relaxed the conscious mind is and the more suggestable you are.

You can turn anything into a deepener. in the inductions previous there are several methods already.

Counting Deepener

Counting as a deepener can be done in several ways

Counting 1

"As I count down from ten to one, you will go ten times deeper, more relaxed and focused with each number. More than ever before.

10 relaxing every muscle, nerve and fibre....9.... 8....going deeper and

deeper.... 7....relaxing further and further....6.... 5....deeper with every heart beat....4....deeper with every breath....2...and..1

as you go deeper, into your hypnosis, the better you will feel. And the better you feel the deeper you will go."

You may have noticed I missed the number 3. This was meant. It confuses the subject and they think did I hear it or not and makes them go even deeper.

Counting 2

"As I count you will go deeper more relaxed into your hypnosis than you ever have before.

10 times deeper, 20 times deeper, 30 times deeper, 40 times, 50 times, 60 times deeper, 70 times deeper, 80, 90 and 100 times deeper more relaxed and focused than ever before."

You can use any counting method you like or make up your own variation of this. This one is very direct and work with people who respond to direct orders (military/police). Id normally use with another probably a visualization deepener.

Visualizing method Stair case.

This is popular with a lot of therapists.

"I'd like you to now use that powerful imagination of yours and visualize standing at the top of a beautiful stair case. Any stair case you like just imagine it.

This stair case has ten stairs, ten stairs going down. And in a moment, but not yet, you're going to walk down the stairs, one step at a time. With each step you will go deeper in to your hypnosis. Twice as deep as you were before.

This stair case can be any stair case you like.

It's your stair case.

Now we are going to start walking down them one step at a time.

Counting backwards from ten.

Ten, step down one step, relaxing and going twice as deep, more relaxed than before.

Nine take another step and relax every muscle nerve and fiber.

Eight going deeper.

Seven Deeper still.

Six twice as deep, deeper.

Five... Four... Three... Two and One even deeper with every breath and every heartbeat.

Visualizing Method Wave

Another popular method.

"I'd like you now to use that powerful imagination of yours. I'd like you to visualize yourself on a beach staring out in to the sea.

It's your beach. It can be anywhere you like. Some where you have been or somewhere you want to go.

And when your there nod.

.......Thank you.

As you stare out to the sea notice that the waves are calm and rhythmic.

coming In and Out, In and Out, notice how calming it is.

In and Out." (it would be good to regulate the waves with the clients breathing)

A FORCE 4 CHANGE

"As the wave comes in, it brings calm and relaxation and as it rolls out it takes away all the tension and stresses of life.

Taking you deeper in to your hypnosis.

In...bringing calm and relaxation, out...taking away all that tension and stress.

going deeper and deeper.

In relaxing more and more. Out releasing all that tension.

That's right."

You can use anything as a deepener even external noises like banging and road noises or people talking etc.

Visualization Numbers method

"In a moment but not yet, I'm going to ask you to count backwards from 100. That's right, count backwards out loud, from 100 down to 1.

With every number, I want you to visualize it, see it and allow it to drift and fade away, completely. And double your relaxation each time.

That's right double your relaxation with every number.

Start now.

100, say it out loud, see it, visualize it, Allow it to fade away, drift away. Double your relaxation.

99, see it, allow it to fade away and relax even further. Now carry on in your own time."

Allow them to carry on occasionally throwing in "that's right relax." And "Deeper more relaxed"

And when you feel they are far enough. It wont take long normally still in the 90's say.

"That's it allow all those numbers to fade and drift away. You don't need them now. Just go deeper with every breath, every heart beat."

You can leave them for a bit if you need to compose yourself for the session. They will happily stay there drifting deeper.

External noises Method

"As you stay there relaxing, going deeper into hypnosis, you may notice some sounds. these sounds are perfectly normal, just life carrying on.

it may be people talking or laughing or just moving around in their day to day life's. its ok, anytime you hear this you will just go deeper more relaxed than ever before.

Every time you hear a bang or a car back fire you will go ten times deeper more relaxed than before.

Drifting sinking deeper more focused than you've ever been before."

As you can see here anything can be turned into a deepener. The only limit is your imagination.

Fractionation

Another good method that during the induction you bring the client round then drop them straight back in again.

This energy shift forces them deeper into trance/hypnosis.

This is known as fractionation. a lot of hypnotists will do this automatically with the following suggestion.

"In a moment but not yet I'm going to ask you to open your eyes. If at any time you hear me say the word Sleep weather your eyes are open or closed you will immediately close your eyes and go ten times deeper more relaxed that before. any time you hear me say sleep you will close your eyes and go ten times deeper than before. when you hear the word sleep you will go ten times deeper more relaxed into hypnosis than before."

This sends them deep very quickly.

Another method based on the energy shift is the hand drop

And this is very quick and easy.

Hand Drop Deepener

"In a moment I'm going to pick your right hand up be the wrist"

Now gently pick the hand up "Give me all the weight. Let me do all the work." gently sway the hand "as your hand drops go ten times deeper more relaxed than before. That's it, give me the weight so it's like a wet rag." now drop the hand on to his lap." deeper than you've ever been."

Now do it again pick up the hand and sway it. If there's any resistance then say to them "let me do all the work." Sway and drop it again "deeper more relaxed."

And repeat one last time

Pick the Hand up and you should have no resistance at all.

"Feel yourself sinking deeper and deeper into hypnosis." drop the hand into his lap.

I use this one every time as well. Its quick and easy and you can see their whole body relax as you drop the hand.

Chapter Six

Suggestions

Now you have them deep in hypnosis
you're ready for suggestion.

But how do you know if the subject is
deep enough?

Well with experience, you will see signs
telling you that you have hypnosis
easily. The novice will easily miss these
signs. If you think you have, or you are
not confidant you may need to do a
convincer. A convincer is only a
suggestion where you or the subject will
realize that something is happening.

You would think that the suggestion phase
is the easy part. well once you have
hypnosis you can give any suggestion you
want right? WRONG

the suggestion phase is actually quite
difficult to master

especially when dealing with sceptics. It
is where a lot of new hypnotists struggle
and give up.

For the suggestion phase to be effective

your pre-talk must be up to scratch. if this is good then the induction and deepeners will be much easier.

You will also need to remember the most forgotten rules of Hypnosis.

You cannot make someone do or say anything against their will.

You need to remember that people are naturally suspicious, and your wording is extremely important when giving suggestions.

Also keep it simple to start with. Go for something easy, then go to progressively more difficult. And compound, the rule of three is good.

Repeat, repeat and repeat again.

What you're doing here is getting compliance with easy simple suggestions.

The more compliance you get the more effective your suggestions will be if that makes sense.

There is a hierarchy of suggestion easy to hard. I've listed the order below.

- change sense (smell/feel/taste)

- catalepsy (the looseness or stiffness or a limb)

- emotion (happy/sad/funny/angry)

- Reduce pain (anesthetic)

- negative hallucination (invisibility)

- positive hallucination (seeing something that isn't there)

You may read the above and think of entertainment.

And you'd be right. Hypnosis has its place in entertainment and that's great for spreading the word about how powerful it is.

I'm going to include towards the end some skits which will allow you to have fun with friends, and have some amazing convincers with clients.

Delivery of suggestion

There are many ways we can deliver a suggestion some are more effective than others for different clients.

It's for the hypnotist to be able to assess the subject and deliver the suggestion the best way for that person.

Methods of suggestion

- Direct suggestion

- Indirect suggestion

- Post hypnotic suggestion

- Parts therapy

- Regression

- Progression

- Metaphor

There are so many ways of giving suggestion

It has to seem effortless, and it has to fit with the client.

I like to mix it up a bit.

I will generally go for a direct method (Make the change now!)

Then maybe add in indirect suggestions.

"How would you feel if this could change? How would you feel if it didn't change?

Which is best for you? And where do you want to be? You can have it now if you want?" get the point. Or "see yourself if

it never changes, are you the same?
Better? or worse? now see yourself having
made those changes. Are you happy with
who you are? and your life?

Do you still want to put the effort in to
get to where you want to be?

Are you willing to put that effort in? to
make the right choices? to be who you
need to be and get to the place you
deserve to be?"

I like to give a visual representation of
what they could be if they do, and if
they don't make whatever changes they
know they need to make. To get where they
want to get to in life, in health or for
whatever reason they have come to me for.

It gives them a boost and that kick up
the arse we all need sometimes.

Metaphor

I love using metaphors as an indirect way
to the subconscious using stories to
activate/captivate the imagination and
hammer home a lesson or point. Milton
Ericson was the master of this.

Though I'm not going to show you
Ericsonian Hypnosis I will give an
example of a metaphor for therapy.

A FORCE 4 CHANGE

My favorite metaphor is this one.

What difference does it make?

Imagine walking along a beach on a beautiful day. The sky is clear the sea is calm and, in the distance, you see a kid throwing pebbles into the calm sea.

You carry on walking. The breeze feels nice against your face.

As you get closer you see that they are not pebbles he's throwing but star fish.

He's surrounded by them. He picks one up and throws it. And then another and another.

You stop him and say

"hey kid what do you think you are doing?"

The kid turns to you

"If these star fish stay on the beach they will dry out and die. I'm saving them."

You look around at all the star fish on the beach and say.

"kid there are thousands of them along this beach. What difference will it make?"

A FORCE 4 CHANGE

The kid turns to you, reaches down to

pick up another star fish and says. "It makes a difference to this one" Then throws it.

I love the story that this metaphor tells. And the message it delivers.

There are so many and you will find ones that you prefer to use to get your point across.

Parts Therapy

Parts therapy is also a brilliant way to communicate with the subconscious. It helps the client know that there is something actually happening beyond their cognitive behavior.

That choices are being made on a subconscious level, and that they can take back control, and then go on to change these behaviors.

Braking the subconscious into its individual parts can be fascinating. It's a bit like multiple personality disorder, especially when you ask each part to literally speak to you.

When using parts therapy, you ask the subject if you can speak to the part of the subconscious that has been

responsible for which ever problem you're dealing with.

For example, let's say a client comes to you that has a compulsive habit, like comfort eating.

When the client is hypnotized, have them positioned with their hands palms up. Make sure the client knows not to assist any movement, or resist any movement. Then ask them.

"I'd like to now speak to johns powerful powerful subconscious. If you're willing to speak to me today, to help john. Can you move any part of johns hands." it helps to gently tap each hand as you say this.

"Please move any part of johns hands, fingers or thumbs now."

Keep a close eye on the hands for any movement.

"John I'd like to remind you not to resist or assist in any movements just allow whatever happens to happen.

To Johns subconscious again. Make any movement so I know your communicating. Can you make the movement bigger so I can see it clearly please?

Thank you."

It sometimes takes a couple of minutes and sometimes it happens straight away.

Sometimes you will ask for a hand but a leg twitches. You just have to adapt.

Also make sure to always thank the subconscious for any response. The subconscious is like a big child it will sulk and ignore you if it doesn't like you.

Now you have a positive response you need to know how to read the movements.

"Thank you for that. Now that your willing to help me can you give me a clear signal for a yes answer. Any movement of a finger or thumb that means Yes! please."

Now wait. You may need to prompt again if it takes too long.

Keep a close eye on the hands it might be a small movement. If you do see one you need to confirm it.

"Thank you. If that is a yes can you show me again please?"

Wait again. It will normally come quicker this time or strait away.

"Thank you"

Again, if you like you can ask for it to be a bigger movement and the subconscious will comply.

"Thank you. Now can you show me a different movement for the answer NO! please."

Now wait again keeping a close eye.

"Thank you."

Again, you need to confirm.

"Again, can you give me the movement that signifies No! please.

Thank you. Can you make it bigger so I can see it clearly? Thank you."

Now you've established communication directly with the subconscious through ideo-motive response using the hands.

Now you need to establish communication with a specific part.

"now I'd like the part of john that has been making john want to eat compulsively. Please can that part talk to me now?"

Look for any movement of the hand especially the yes or no response.

"Can I speak to that part now please."

Keep waiting it can take a minute.

When you see a movement ask for confirmation.

"If you're the part that's responsible for the compulsive eating please can you give a signal for yes?"

You will see a positive movement.

"Thank you. I know you've been helping john and I thank you for that. And I know john appreciates you help.

Do you still want to help john?"

Wait for the yes response. If you get a no you will need to reword the question. Remember that the subconscious can act like a spoilt child. But we will assume all is fine here.

"Thank you that's great Thank you" you need to constantly big up the ego.

"You've Done a great job up to now. But the eating is not helping john anymore, it's doing the opposite. And I know you don't want to hurt john do you." wait for the response.

"Can we stop the compulsive eating and replace it with something to help john? This way you still have a job and you can keep helping john." wait for the response

Parts generally want to help. They don't like being without a role which is why the behavior which may have started to help john feel better carried on after it was needed.

You can discuss with the client beforehand what they would like to do but can't get the motivation to do. Or what they would like to replace the habit with. Then it's just a matter of asking the part to help in a different way.

You will be amazed at the results.

Regression

There are many different reasons to do regression. Some therapists think regression to cause is necessary to deal with trauma. Where others think regression to cause is just unnecessary and only serves to retraumatize the client.

I'm from the latter camp that believe regression to cause isn't necessary. Why put the client through the memory again? I believe the subconscious knows why it's doing what it does. And it does it to protect you and all you have to do is show it that it is not helping you anymore and give it an alternative positive behavior. If you take something away always put something nice back or the old habit will return or another bad thing might take its place.

That said a client might come in and request a regression to a lost memory

Or really wants to know why a certain behavior started so progression to cause might be needed then.

It's actually easy to do. We will do a regression to cause.

"As you carry on drifting deeper and deeper. Focus on my voice.

That's right!

I want you to focus on that feeling of anxiety, think about that feeling now.

Think about how you feel when it gets bad now think about it knowing your safe and everything is ok.

I want you to remember back to the last time you felt that feeling the anxiety.

Remember the last time it happened now. Your safe here I just want you to remember it. go there now.

You are safe, see it as a memory as a by stander you can't be hurt.

And when you are there nod.

Thank you."

Right here keep a close eye on the client. If they start to panic you will need to step in and calm them down.

And make sure they are safe because you don't know what situation you are making them remember.

"I want you to tell me what you see?

Where are you?

What's around you?

Do you know the date?

Who is with you?"

This is where you gather as much information as you can. Write it down so you can confirm it later or come back to it in the future

That was the last time they felt anxiety. It's the easiest to remember. And remember to tell them they are safe and just observing not actually experiencing the anxiety all over again.

You may get an abreaction which is an

unexpected response to the traumatic event but stay calm and steer them back to calmness.

Now take them back to the time before that.

"Thank you for that.

I want you to go back further I'm going to count backwards from 3 to one and when I reach one you will be at a time and date before the last when you felt this anxiety. When I count back to one you will be at an earlier time where you felt this anxiety."

Now go through the questions again. Remember to take notes.

I would do this two or three times, and then ask to go to the first time they felt this anxiety and remember to go through the questions again.

Once at the root cause you can then disassociate the anxiety from the situation then get rid all together.

You disassociate the feeling quite easily. A popular method is the cinema method.

"I want you to recall this event again but this time I want you to watch it, as if you were watching it unfold on a movie screen, in a cinema. That's right the whole event is on the screen.

See yourself, the people you are with, watch the whole seen unfold like a movie

See how you react, watch how you stand, how you speak, how you deal with the situation.

How do you feel watching back now?

What would you say to that version of you now?

Good.

Now I want you to rewind the event like a video, and pause it at the beginning.

Good.

Now I want you to press play.

I want you now to take another step back and watch the other version of you watch the screen. That's right watch the other version of you as you watch the event on the screen.

How is that version of you acting?

What is your posture as you watch the events unfold on video?

How do you look while watching that video?

How do you feel, about seeing how you react to watching the video?

How do you feel now, about that event on the video?

Now what would you say to that you?"

Now you have disassociated the event from the feeling, or at least desensitized the event. Now you can replace it with love and confidence.

Remember if you remove something then replace it with something nice.

You will see examples of progression where you make the client see themselves in the future having not changed and then again having made changes. It is a good way to give motivation to change.

You can even go to past life regression or future life progression that's a bit more specialist and I think an idea for another book lol.

Chapter Seven

Convincers

Convincers help you gauge the depth, but it also convinces the client that something is happening.

Use the hierarchy in your convincers. This also helps for deepening.

It works like fractionation. To bring them round have a convincer then drop them back in again is even more powerful it takes them deeper every time you do it and helps the client believe something is fundamentally happening.

Convincers

A convincer is exactly that. it's a suggestion that convinces the client that something is happening, convinces the client that they are hypnotized.

Below are the standard convincers you will come across, and are very affective.

EYE LOCK

This is a really good convincer and is used in the Dave Elman induction.

"As you sit there relaxing deeper and deeper I want you to focus your attention on your eyes.

That's right, I want you to relax all those tiny muscles around your eyes.

all those little muscles relaxing more and more until your eyes are so relaxed that they just won't open.

relaxing those tiny muscles so much that they just don't work.

I want you to use that powerful imagination of yours now, and imagine that the most powerful super glue is gluing your eyes shut, tight shut, stuck shut

the most powerful glue you can imagine is sticking tight, stuck tight, glued tight. Sticking, gluing, stuck tight. And when you know you can't open them just try!

Try and only try to open your eyes and realize that they just won't open!

And the more you try the more stuck they become.

And now relax. And go even deeper."

A FORCE 4 CHANGE

So that's the eye lock convincer it's
good to use in the induction such as Dave
Elman does. Its relatively easy to
achieve.

It gives you confidence in your ability
in your early career used as a depth
test. After a while you will see other
signs micro movements flushing etc. You
won't need to test your work and it
becomes a convincer for the client.

ARM LOCK

"As you carry on drifting deeper and
deeper with each breath I want you to
hold your arm out in front of you"

Now you can take either of their hands
and bring it up in front of them, and
tell them to hold it there palm down, and
close their fist.

"Hold your arm out here in front of you
palm down, and keep your fist tight.

And as you carry on relaxing I want you
to use that amazing imagination of yours
that amazing imagination of yours.

Imagine that your arm is getting stiffer
and stronger like a bar of steal. Locking
at the elbow rigid and stiff like a bar
of steal

A FORCE 4 CHANGE

Welded to you shoulder.

Its stiff and rigid strong like a bar of steal welded to your shoulder."

Now tap gently on the arm from the wrist to the shoulder and back down again as you continue saying

"Stiffer, Stronger, Tighter, stronger tighter stiffer. Like one bar of steal."

Pressing down to the floor gently allowing it to spring back to its original position.

"Tighter, stiffer, rigid like a solid bar of steal, that's good."

Now cup your hand around their fist.

"I want you to make this so stiff so strong that even I can't bend it"

Now push in from the fist towards the shoulder.

"That's good, so stiff, stiffer, so rigid like one bar of steal. Stiffer, Stronger, Stiffer.

So rigid now. That when you know you can't bend it, just try, and see that you can't...Now stop.

As you now sink deeper into hypnoses relax that arm and allow it to slowly drift back to your side, and sink even deeper.

That's right"

The Arm Lock convincer is a powerful one. If your client locks their arm and can't bend or lower the arm they will believe completely and sink even deeper into hypnosis. And changes can be made even easier.

A lot of Convincers will focus around catalepsy which is really easy to achieve in hypnosis.

Catalepsy being the stiffness or looseness of a muscle or group of muscles.

Sticking someone's feet to the floor so they can't move, or their hand to their head or a table are also really good ones to use

Feet Rooted to the Floor

Remember this is after the whole Pre-talk Induction, and deepeners.

"As you carry on drifting deeper and deeper I want you to concentrate entirely on your feet.

As you focus on your feet, imagine that

your legs are like tree trunks, and your feet are the roots

Imagine and only imagine that your feet are rooted in to the floor

Your feet are rooted deep into the floor and you can't move them. The more you try the deeper the roots go and the more stuck they become.

You can't move your feet because they are rooted solid into the floor.

Now try to move them and notice them getting stuck tighter as the roots go deeper,"

Now you can open their eyes and get them to try to move their feet.

"3...2...1… Now Open your eyes and notice that you can't move your feet. Now try and notice they are stuck, and the more you try the more stuck they are. That's Good now Sleep and go deeper."

You can do this with the hand on a table or wall or on their own head. Instead or roots you can use the strongest glue in the world or even cement.

The only limit is your imagination.

Chapter Eight

Emergence

The emergence is the last part. When done right it will leave the subject feeling fantastic and wanting more.

There are loads of different ways to emerge someone. And you will find your favorite or even make your own up.

I will show a couple of simple ones and then an energetic method so you can choose your favorite.

Count back from 3

Easy simple and not much to it.

"In a moment I'm going to count back from three down to one and when I reach one you will wake up from hypnosis. No longer hypnotized, feeling amazing. Three...two...one open your eyes feeling absolutely amazing."

Count themselves up

Evan easier than the first.

"in a moment I want you to count yourself
up from one to three. When you reach
three you will awake from hypnosis
feeling great. Count up in your own time
now."

The risk with this one is that they don't
wake themselves up because you say in
your own time. Most people enjoy hypnosis
so much that they don't want to wake
themselves from it. You might be waiting
a while.

If this is the case, then say the
following.

"Count your self up now"

If this doesn't work then say.

"If you don't bring yourself out of
hypnosis now you will never go in again."

Now there is no truth to this but the
threat is enough.

Energetic method.

This method has a bit more energy in your
voice.

"In a moment I'm going to bring you out of hypnosis when I do you will be wide awake, full of energy ready to face the world and carry on stronger and full of confidence.

One. feel yourself getting less and less relaxed.

Two. take a nice big breath and fill your lungs with beautiful fresh air.

Three. feel a rush of energy as the blood pumps through your vanes.

Four. waking more a more confidant.

Five. open your eyes feeling fully refreshed full of confidence, full of strength."

Stage Hypnosis Emergence

For stage Hypnosis remember that you have been filling their subconscious up with fun entertaining suggestions. We need to remove these.

"In a moment I'm going to wake you up from hypnosis and when I do you will no longer be hypnotized. and all suggestions given to you will no longer be effective. No suggestions that you had while hypnotized on this stage will be effective."

You can be specific with the suggestions
you want to remove if there were any good
ones that would benefit them.

1 becoming less and less relaxed

2 feeling a rush of energy as it surges
through your body.

3 clear your lungs as you take a nice
deep breath.

4 All suggestions removed. Starting to
come out of hypnosis now.

5 Open your eyes. No longer hypnotized

Chapter Nine
Force 4 Change

Hypnosis can be used for many many things. From stress relief to controlling birthing pain.

Here I'm going to concentrate on the 4 area's listed in the beginning

- Mental health

- Diet

- Physical

- Spiritual

I believe that each of these areas affect the other.

And that only working on one area and neglecting the rest will result in a relapse or even a whole new disorder or situation arising.

There are many things that fall in to

these categories especially mental health.

The first to look at is Anxiety and stress

This is easy to deal with through hypnosis and is one of the most common things a hypnotherapist is likely to deal with.

So, remember to get your client/subject completely ready

Ensure they are ready to make the change.

Find out the what and the why. Find out what they would like most. Remember if we remove something put something nice back in. so what do they want most.

Carry out a full pre-talk, a Yes set, compliance set, the induction, deepeners and even test with convincers.

Now you are ready to carry out some real change work. Remember to observe closely.

Look out for any minor reactions, micro-movements.

Movements of the eyes or fingers the tiny facial muscles.

These can be a sign that the subconscious is trying to communicate with you. Or a sign that the subconscious is busy making changes.

You will learn to read these with experience.

Stress and Anxiety

First, I would do a mental detox to get rid of any thing that has been affecting them in general over the recent days, weeks or months or even years that may cloud the mind over the root cause.

Mental detox

I use this with every client. It gets rid of any junk that's in their heads, that might cloud their mind, and stop/block them from making the changes needed.

"In a moment I'm going to count down from 5 down to one, and when I reach one you will be in a place where you can make some perfect positive changes. A mystical magical place. Your place. Any place you would like to be.

5 going deeper more relaxed than ever before going to your mystical magical place.

4 getting closer.

3 almost there, that mystical magical place.

2 and 1 standing in that mystical magical place where you can make those changes.

Ready to change your life for the better.

As you stand there, know that your perfectly safe. Because this is your place.

Look around, and get to know this place.

This is your place. No that at any time you can come back here. You are perfectly safe here.

I want you to notice now that there's a beautiful bright white light above your head.

Notice that this light is getting brighter and brighter.

And its pulling and tugging on any negative feelings, thoughts and emotions, that you have had over the last few days, weeks, months or years.

Its pulling and tugging on all the negative feelings, thoughts and emotions now. Feel them coming out like a weight being lifted off the top of your head, off your shoulders now.

Feel that negativity leaving your body

now.

Give yourself permission to let go now.

Feel all that hurt, pain, anger and shame disappear.

As that light starts to drift down now and come closer. Feel it as it pulls stronger and stronger.

As it gets closer and closer just let it go.

Let it all go now.

As that light starts to pass through you now allow it to take all the residual hurt and pain anger and shame.

Taking every little bit now as it passes down in to your neck and chest. Feel the calming sensation, as it comes over as it all gets taken away now.

Drifting down through your torso, your hips and thighs, and out through your feet and toes.

And relax."

Now the mental detox is done. For some people this would be good enough to relieve stress and anxiety, but we will assume that its deeper rooted than this.

Stress & Anxiety

After the Mental Detox, bring them round and ask if anything popped up, any images feeling thoughts or emotions that they were or weren't expecting.

And if it was anything to do with the problem they are having? And how are they feeling about it now?

Then when you have the information or not as the case may be.

Ask the client to simply close their eye and sleep deepening them again.

Just because you asked them to open their eyes, doesn't mean that they are out of hypnosis.

Earlier remember giving them the instruction, that if you say the command "Sleep" whether they have their eyes open or closed it would send them deeper in to hypnosis. This is why.

You can use any deepener you like. Or even make one up.

Here is another visualization.

"I want you to imagine a chalk board in front of you with chalk and a board rubber. Pick up the chalk in one hand, and the rubber in your other.

A FORCE 4 CHANGE

When you have them nod...good.

Now with the chalk I want you to draw the letter A on the board. When you have done it nod...Good

With the other hand I want you to rub it out using the board rubber, and drift 10 times deeper.

When you've done that nod...Good

And drift ten times deeper more relaxed than ever before.

Now the letter B . . .

When you've done that rub it out and drift ten times deeper.

...That's right.

Now carry on through the alphabet drifting deeper and deeper with every letter."

You can leave then for a minute while they take themselves deeper.

"now you can stop writing now. It doesn't matter just carry on going deeper with every breath and every heartbeat.

I want you now to focus on that thing that causes the anxiety and stress. Focus on it now, see it, feel it, but your perfectly safe and perfectly fine. See it now, but as a bystander see it for what it is. Notice your reaction to it. Notice the change in your body in your face.

Notice as the feeling changes it's no longer affecting you in the same way. It's still there but it's different. Its ok to be aware of it but there's no need to stress or be scared of it. Its ok to be weary but you can learn from it and adapt to be a better you.

You are strong! you are strong! That's right learn from it, don't let it take control. You are in control.

Learn from it and use it.

Become stronger! You are stronger!

The more you think about that thing the stronger you feel!

And the stronger, you feel the better you feel!

I want your amazing subconscious to lock these changes in.

And when you know that change is made open your eyes."

Now get more feedback, you can always go back in and make more changes if there were other things that popped up.

You can target things specifically. Get them to focus on a feeling an event or even a situation.

Other things that can be worked with for mental health are confidence and self-esteem.

There are several methods when dealing with self-esteem and confidence.

Confidence and self esteem

A lack of confidence generally comes from a fear of failing or being ridiculed so work on it from one or both of these angles.

Talk to them about a good working ethic. A be prepared approach to everything they do. The 6 P's Prior Preparation Prevents Piss Poor Performance. Do this with everything you do and there is no need to be scared of failing. To fail knowing you have done your best isn't failing.

"Sleep, and go deeper and deeper. Remember the feeling from earlier, relaxing, drifting even deeper."

Pick up the wrist

"let me have all the weight"

Drop the wrist in their lap from 6 inches

"Sleep and go deeper more relaxed"

Pick up the wrist again and drop in to the lap again.

"sleep deeper more relaxed than before."

And one more time pick up the Wrist and drop again.

"sleep go even deeper relaxing every muscle, every fiber.

I want you to go back to your place where you can make those positive changes. That mystical magical place. The place that's just for you now.

When your there just nod.

Good.

I'd like your powerful subconscious to take you to a control room, it's your control room with levers switches dials.

I want you to find the lever that controls your confidence.

Turn it all the way up to full now feel how it feels to be all the way up to full. That feeling of being full of confidence.

A FORCE 4 CHANGE

Enjoy that feeling, imaging what you can achieve.

Make that lever stay there now.

Lock it, chain it, weld it in place

You know now that you are a confidant person, that person you need to be. The Person that can achieve anything he/she sets their mind on.

Confidence comes with knowledge and being prepared. So, remember now that you will be prepared to do whatever you need to.

And if you need to, you know you can always prepare yourself for any situation.

Because you know you can do it. You will do it. You can do it you will do it.

Prepare for anything you need to, and be confidant you have done all you can.

Remember Prior Preparation Prevents Piss Poor Performance.

Prior Preparation Prevents Piss Poor Performance.

Prior Preparation Prevents Piss Poor Performance.

I want your powerful subconscious now to lock that in.

It's now yours, because you can do it, and will do it.

And when you know those changes are made you can open your eyes"

That's two techniques in one session the Control room method combined with direct suggestion. I like to do this to strengthen the session.

Diet/Weight loss

Why Diet and weight loss or management? Well this goes to Mindset and health the fitter we are in body and mind the easier it will be to make lasting changes.

We will feel better and healthier and in a better position to achieve those life changing goals.

Also, if you have a bad diet you will have less energy and feel bloated. Or to much energy or caffeine in your system at bed time. It all has an effect on our mind set

"as you drift deeper with every breath go back to your mystical, magical place. The place where you can make perfect, positive changes. Go there now.

And when your there, nod.

Good

Now what I want is your powerful imagination to imagine a table. I want you to imagine all your favorite foods on this table. All the foods you would normally eat on that table. See them there in front of you. Your favorite meals, deserts, take away's.

Now I want you to imagine all the unhealthy foods on that table gone.

The sugary, fatty foods that you know are bad for you.

All those sugary, fatty, salty foods.

Make them disappear now.

Now look at that table.

See what's left. Isn't that depressing.

Dieting isn't about depriving food. Because if you are not allowed something, then you want it, you crave it.

You know what food is healthy. Now imagine the foods you like that are healthy on the table. See them there now.

If no food is forbidden then there's

nothing to crave.

I want your powerful subconscious now to reconnect with your stomach. Feel the senses, the signals now as your stomach communicates with you.

Feel every nerve fiber as you feel what your gut is trying to tell you.

Eat when you need to! Don't eat when you don't!

It's that simple.

You don't need to eat big meals only eat when you are hungry. Eat the good foods and snack on healthy foods you know what they are good for you.

Listen to your gut and take note.

Treats are ok to. But if you are not hungry wait, save it.

You know what's good for you and what's not.

Eat when you need to when you are hungry. Not when you are bored.

You can do it, and will do it.

Now make the changes you need to, to eat healthy, feel healthy.

Now know you are in control. Eat what you

want when you want when you need to.

You can do it! You will do it! You can do it! You will do it!"

Physical health

Using Hypnosis to help with Physical health and fitness is actually quite common.

You may be thinking but how is it going to make me fit and healthy? It's Not, You Are!

Hypnosis is a tool to help you meet your goals. It will help motivate you. Alter your mind set to focus on your physical and health goals. It can make it easier for you to achieve them.

Most of us have said "I need to sign up to a Gym" not many of us do. And out of those of us that do, a big portion of us don't dedicate the time to going, as we should if at all.

But if I said There is a Million pound waiting for you. All you have to do is get to your peak fitness by the end of 12 months and run a marathon in under 3 hours.

I know if someone said that to me I'd be changing my diet and working out every

second I can until I get to that goal,
and claim my million pounds.

It's a matter of motivation. Change your
mind set, and make the goals realistic
and reachable. Then see what benefits you
can have. It might not be the million
pounds, but living longer and healthier,
feeling good, looking good are all
achievable. Liking what you look like and
living life, rather than just watching it
go by because it seems like too much
effort. Actually, have fun with life.

Physical Health

"As you carry on drifting, relaxing,
focusing on my voice I'd like you now, to
go to your place that special, private
place, where you can make those perfect
positive changes in your life today. It's
your place, a magical, mystical place.

Go there now...Good!

As you relax in this place, where your
perfectly safe, perfectly fine.

I want you now to focus. Focus on you and
your body.

I want you to focus on that now.

Focus on the body you have, and the body

you want.

It might be the same, it may be different. if different, How?

Focus on it now.

How would it feel to be fitter, feel fitter, feel good about your body, feeling great, feeling healthy? You can do this, you will do this.

Get fitter, get healthier feel great.

You need to work hard to get the body you deserve. But its only hard if you don't want it. But you do want it! And you will do it.

You want to be fitter. You want to look great. You want to feel great. And enjoy it. It feels good to get fit, look fit, be fit.

You can do it you will do it.

Walk when you can.

Jog when you can, or ride your bike when you can.

Make the little changes, when you can, to make the changes you want.

To achieve what you want, and feel great.

Eat healthy, be healthy, live healthy, feeling fantastic.

A FORCE 4 CHANGE

I want you to now imagine yourself ten years from now doing what you do now, feeling like you've always felt, living like you've always lived.

Imagine that now. Imagine if you don't make those changes. Where you will end up? How you will end up?

See what you are doing? how you look? and how you feel?

Has your health suffered? or not changed? has your body changed?

Has your mental health changed? Do you feel OK?

Now, I want you to now imagine yourself ten years from now, having made those changes. Eating healthier, making those small changes to live healthier, move more, go for walks, Jogging, bike rides, or even join a gym. See yourself now having made all those choices to change now to be the healthier fitter you. That feels great, looks great. That loves and lives life to the fullest.

See that person now.

Know you can be that person! You are that person! You can achieve whatever you set your mind on and if you want this it's yours.

Make those changes to motivate yourself, to be the best version of you.

You can do it! you will do it! you can do it! you will do it!

Do it now and lock those changes in place, and be the best version of you that you can be now.

It's not hard work if you enjoy it! and you will enjoy every minute of life! and all its challenges! Live your life on your terms!

And feel fantastic."

You can chop and change this for personal goals. For either medical or fitness changes. Feeling healthy, feeling fit and liking what we look like all link to feeling good about ourselves. It all links in with mental health. I believe that to really heal ourselves we need to love ourselves, and if we are honest sometimes we don't even like our selves.

So, we've looked at mental wellbeing, diet, and physical health now we come to spiritual.

I believe this is one key component that most programs fail on.

Yes, they may work on the short term. But

are they sustainable over the long term?

As people we are easily distracted. One event can knock us completely off course. Then another knocks us again and again. If we have nothing to calm the mind and refocus the mind. Then one day you may wake up not even realizing that you have completely changed how you are living. Not realizing that you have neglected your diet. Your health. Your fitness.

Don't get me wrong we are not machines, we can't always be focused 100% of the time.

But if we can calm, and refocus the mind, yes there may be new goals, new priorities but we can deal with them and still live and enjoy living.

Feeling good about our choices and why we make them.

That's living the life we deserve.

Spiritual health

As you Carry on drifting, floating, relaxing, focusing on my voice.

I want you to go to that place, your place. where you can make perfect positive changes in life.

A FORCE 4 CHANGE

A mystical place. A magical place where you can be safe.

Where you can relax and focus.

Go there now.

Go there, and relax, drift, go deeper and deeper as you listen and focus sinking drifting relaxing deeper and deeper.

Deeper with every breath, every heartbeat.

It feels so good to be there and the better you feel the deeper you go.

As you carry on drifting deeper, have a look around this place your place.

Get comfortable your safe here.

You can focus here.

You can relax here.

It feels so good here.

You can come here any time you like. Whenever you like.

When you need to feel calm and focused. Just take three deep breaths all the way in and all the way out. Close your eyes and relax. Use that powerful imagination of yours to bring yourself here.

You can relax here. You can focus here.

A FORCE 4 CHANGE

You can concentrate here.

Any time you want to come back here, just take three deep breaths, close your eyes and relax.

That's right and relax from the top of your head to the tips of your toes. See a wave of relaxation as it passes down, then come here.

Here you can refocus and calm your mind. Or just relax and feel refreshed. It's your place it's all up to you. Stay for as long as you like. For as long as you need.

You are in control, and you feel amazing, you are in control of your own destiny! you are in control!"

That's the final part of the puzzle.

Be comfortable with yourself, happy with your diet, health and fitness.

Be able to stay calm and focused even after the most difficult times.

Live life to the fullest with no regrets.

And the world is your oyster.

Just remember to have some me time where you can focus on you! Center yourself! Refresh yourself.

Could be a hobby you can get lost in. x

Chapter Ten

Uses of Hypnosis

Stop Smoking / Smoking Cessation

For smoking cessation to be effective the client has to really want to stop smoking.

If he/she is under pressure from family, friends or the Dr then you will have less of a chance of success.

The reason is they don't really want to stop. Either because they enjoy it. It calms them down or they like the socialness.

And even if the hypnosis is working, they can easily pick up a cigarette again and start. Because they didn't want to stop in the first place.

If they come to you and really do want to stop, then you can strengthen the desire by imbedding the benefits.

Ask "so why do you want to stop? Good.

So how many a day do you smoke on a normal day?"

A FORCE 4 CHANGE

Here we will assume 20 its normal for someone who wants to quit, to smoke at least this much.

Ok, so I assume it can be more on a bad day? Yes.

So, working on 20 per day the average cost is £10 a day? Yes

That's £70 a week, roughly £300 a month or £3650 a year. Sounds about right?

What would another £3650 at the end of the year mean to you and your family?

It's a brilliant family holiday, or even a car.

How's your health?

Ok so do you get breathless easily? Do you walk much?

How would it feel if you could walk more and not get so breathless?

Play with the kids more? go out more? wouldn't that be great?

If you did give up now you'd probably extend your life expectancy for a few more years. What would that mean to you? See the kids grow up maybe even the grand kids?

So, we've established you would benefit

financially by £3650 per year

You'd be healthier and fitter so be able to play with the kids more and do more.

You will be able to live longer and see your kids grow up and maybe the grand kids.

All these benefits, doesn't that sound fantastic?

Are you still happy to give up?"

Now, go through the whole hypnosis cycle Pre-talk including yes and compliance set. Induction and deepeners. Regress back to the first taste.

"I'd like you to think about your fist ever cigarette, that's right the first fag.

Think about that first taste that first drag. The first instant that smoke hit the back of the mouth. Taste it now. Taste it.

Feel how it felt as that disgusting taste hits the back of your throat, that sickening smoke. Gagh Gagh"

make the gagging noise to emphasize the suggestion.

"I want you now to imagine that taste getting stronger more disgusting, Gagh.

now getting stronger and stronger and that gagging feeling that horrible gagging nasty smoke taste, Gagh, getting stronger again.

It's so disgusting you want to be sick. Gagh

Every time you think about having a smoke this taste will come back.

And get even stronger. That disgusting sickening feeling will be back.

You don't need them anymore.

You don't want them.

Each time you think about them you want to throw up. Gagh"

This is an effective way to stop someone smoking. And acting out the gagging noise can be fun too.

Pain Control

There are many reasons for Pain control including Birthing. Getting a tattoo, Arthritis and many more. The easiest way to achieve this is by asking them to imagine the let's say the hand getting numb as if it plunged into ice cold water like it was submerged in ice. Getting number and number like it's in

112

ice cold freezing water.

Another way is to relax them and calm and use direct suggestion to block the communication between the pain receptors and the brain so there's no pain at all. That there will be no feeling at all in that area just a numbing feeling no pain just numbness like a powerful anesthetic has been injected just a numbing absolutely no pain.

Phobias

This is a common one I see all the time its normally an irrational fear.

As an example, let's say a fear of spiders. There are many ways to do this but I'm going to use white light therapy.

"I want you to go to your safe place that place that's special to you. Where you can make some positive changes today.

Good Now as you stand there in your safe place that special place know that no harm can come to you.

I want you to think of that fear of spiders. Think about it now. As if a spider was in front of you allow that feeling to come up now.

Your perfectly safe.

113

I want you now to imagine that powerful
white light above your head now.

Getting brighter and brighter. As it gets
brighter feel it tugging on that fear
pulling that fear right out of you feel
it pulling and tugging, tugging and
pulling that fear right out of you now
until it's no longer there.

That fear is no longer there feel it
coming off like a weight of your
shoulders now disappearing in to the
light."

Now back fill with confidence and self-
love. Or anything else nice.

White light therapy works for loads of
different things and it's easy to
remember.

Other things you can use hypnosis for
include but not limited to Depression,
Confidence, Insomnia, Nail biting,
Stammer, Sexual Performance, Pain, Past
Lives, Future Lives, Life between Lives.

Depression.

As a Hypnotist you are not a Dr so you
cannot take a client off medication. U

If you have a client is depressed then
Hypnotherapy can almost certainly help

them. But if your client is clinically depressed and on anti-depressants you can still work with them but its best done in conjunction with the client's Dr or at least with them in the know. You should also tell your client to seek advice from their Dr first especially before even thinking of coming off the medication. These anti-depressants will most certainly have side effects if suddenly stopped.

Confidence.

Seeing a hypnotist for lack of confidence is common and is easily. Your likely to hear I want to be more confident but what does that really mean. Unless you know why they need to be confidant you will have little effect.

For example, they might really mean "I want to be less shy" or "I'd like to put my point across in a discussion without worrying about what others think".

Or "I want to be able to take a test without going to pieces"

If you know why they need to be confident then you will be able to target that area and have more affect.

Insomnia.

This one is easy. Relaxation is a byproduct of hypnosis and you can use it to teach relaxation. By going through the progressive muscle relaxation, yourself becoming so relaxed will help calm the mind and help you easily fall asleep.

Nail biting.

This is usually a learnt behavior to ease nerves that's turned in to a habit or to relieve boredom. You can use parts therapy on this or maybe habit reversal therapy.

Habit reversal is when you identify the unwanted habit and get the client to recognize when the urge to do it occurs. Then replace it with a much more pleasant action until the urge for the old habit disappears.

Stammer

This normally would stem from self-esteem and confidence. Usually stemming from a childhood trauma. Performing a regression to cause and helping the client see there's nothing to be afraid of. Use a disassociation technique and help them know that they can now move on with confidence.

Also, while completely relaxed under hypnosis asking the client to repeat words that they would normally have difficulty with.

Sexual performance

If there is not a medical reason then it most certainly can be helped with hypnosis. And a lot of the problem will be self-esteem and confidence. Or performance anxiety. What you will find is that the client may be reluctant to talk to a member of the opposite sex or vice versa.

Pain.

There are two main types of pain. Psychosomatic pain or pain with a physical cause. Both can be helped with hypnosis. Once you have hypnotized the client and numbed the pain using hypnosis usually by numbing the pain with a cold sensation. You can help the client with post hypnotic suggestions to be able to create the same pain relief with self-hypnosis.

Majority of things that people see a hypnotist for boils down to self-esteem and confidence.

I'm not including scripts for all of these because the only script is the client. During your pretalk and pre-session questions you should get all the information you need to help the client. And do it using direct and indirect suggestion, Control room, metaphor, Parts or white light therapy the choice is yours.

You might even invent your own method. If you do you can make a fortune teaching it to other hypnotists.

Chapter Eleven
Stage or Street
Hypnosis

When doing Hypnosis for street and stage, you still have to go through the Hypnosis cycle.

Recap

pretalk including yes set and compliance

Induction.

Deepeners.

Suggestion. (the fun stuff)

Emergence. remembering to remove all suggestions

The one difference you will see in a stage show to street hypnosis is that the hypnotist will do a suggestibility test.

This test is to show the hypnotist who is more suggestable than the rest.

On the down side it also feeds the myth
that only weak-willed people can be
hypnotized.

It gets rid of the members of the crowd,
that will resist no matter what. It also
gives the guys that just don't want to be
hypnotized, a get out clause. If you just
ask for volunteers you will get all sorts
of people.

The ones that get bullied into it by
friends and family. They won't be good
subjects.

The members that will try and prove that
they can't be hypnotized, because they
are strong of will. You don't want them
either.

By testing, you will identify the 20%
that are very easy to hypnotize, and will
make a good show.

The tests I'm going to show you are,
magnetic fingers and sticky hands. And
there is a good reason for both.

The first test I would choose is either
the magnetic fingers or light and heavy

"Please everyone stand and hold your
hands out in front of you, with finger
interlocked.

With the rest of the fingers locked Point

both index fingers up to the sky, with a gap of 1 inch.

Now I want you to imagine a magnet on each tip as you focus on those fingers, pulling and tugging those fingers together.

Imagine the magnets getting stronger and stronger and they can't resist the hypnosis magnets pull."

Try this test yourself. You'll find that the fingers will come together naturally. So, the people who sit down don't want to be hypnotized or want to prove that they are always in control and will fight you every step.

Now say to the crowd. "Now everyone whose fingers came together stay standing, and everyone else please sit down, I can't use you tonight, thank you. Enjoy the show.

Everyone else whose left standing, I need to whittle it down a bit more."

The guys left standing that don't know that it's natural for the fingers to come together think you're a wizard. Now I'd go straight to sticky hands.

"Those of you left standing id like you to hold your hands out in front of you, again fingers interlocked just as before, but all fingers locked tight.

Now look at your hands and fingers locked tight and close your eyes.

Take a nice deep breath and relax every other part of your body.

Just focus on your hands and fingers locking them tight.

I want you now to imagine your hands are glued stuck together.

Stuck tight, like the most powerful super glue is sticking your hands together.

Tighter and tighter.

Imagine that your hands are welded together like one solid bar of steel.

Tighter and tighter and tighter.

Stuck tight like one solid bar of steel.

Imagine them sticking as they get tighter and tighter.

More stuck. Solid like a bar of solid steel.

Now put your hands above your head.

The more you try to pull them apart the more stuck they are.

Sticking, stuck, tight."

A FORCE 4 CHANGE

Watch the crowd closely and see who's struggling and see who can't pull them apart.

Ask all that couldn't pull them apart to join you on stage and you will separate their hands for them. If you have got this then guess what they are already hypnotized because the only thing holding their hands together, was your suggestion. Or if everyone could separate them say something like. "as I watched I saw that some of you found it harder than normal to pull your hands apart. If you did stay standing"

Remember you were watching for good subjects. If you saw someone that had stuck hands then call them up.

"everyone that comes up. Don't worry you can't be made to do anything you don't want to do but I promise you that you will feel relaxed and refreshed as if you had slept for a full 8 hours"

Now use an induction like the eye fixation induction in the induction section of this book.

Street

As a recap we will go through the whole cycle. And we can do it as if we have just stopped someone in the street.

Pretalk

"Have you been hypnotized before? A yes is good but assume no

what do you know about hypnosis?

Good well let me tell you about it. Your subconscious is amazing and Hypnosis is away to unlock its power.

Most people think that only the week minded can be hypnotized but the truth is anyone with above normal intelligence can be hypnotized.

And it's not about losing control either. You can't be made to do anything against your will. It's just not possible.

So, in the same instance I can't make you tell me your deepest darkest secrets. You won't say or do anything you don't want to. Makes sense?

Good

You may hear me say words like sleep or deeper, but you are never actually asleep. Relaxation is a side effect so at best you will just be deeply relaxed

You will be aware of everything going on around you. You will hear everything feel and sense everything. You will just be completely focused.

So, are you ready to see just how powerful your subconscious is and feel amazing?

Great.

Take my hand. Good.

Stand over here. good

Place your feet shoulder width apart. That's it.

Let me have all the weight of this hand. Make it loose and limp like a rag.

That's it.

Focus here on this point between my eyes. Just here right between my eyes.

Don't take your eyes off this spot here. That's it.

Focus your eyes completely on that spot."

Shake the hand gently to make sure you have all the weight.

"Good. I want you to focus on your breathing. Breathing all the way in and all the way out."

Match their Breathing.

"that's right all the way in. And all the way out. Relaxing with every breath.

Breathing relaxation. Breath out tension.

Carry on breathing just as deep as is comfortable. That's right.

Notice now how heavy your eyes are getting. As that hypnosis starts to trickle in to your eyelids now.

Feel your eyes getting heavier and heavier.

Notice now as you blink the heavier they get. And the heavier they get the more you want to close them but not yet.

In a moment I'm going to say the word sleep and when I do you will close your eyes and go ten times deeper more relaxed than before.

When I say sleep whether your eyes are open or closed you will close your eyes and go ten times deeper than ever before.

Now Sleep!" Say this firmly and loud, with a short sharp tug on the hand your holding. You will notice the subject slump and if you get what is known as a flopper they may fall so be ready to catch them. Or before the tug say

"when I say sleep you will remain standing safe a secure. Your legs are strong like tree trunks when a say the word sleep you will go ten times deeper

relaxed but remain standing. Sleep."
again say it loud and sharp as you tug on
the hand.

Now deepen.

"Go Ten times deeper, twenty times
deeper, thirty times deeper."

Drop the hand gently to the side and say
deeper more relaxed.

"Forty, fifty, sixty times deeper"

Again, pick up and drop a hand.

"seventy, eighty, ninety and one hundred
times deeper. Drifting deeper with ever
heart beat every breath."

Now you have them deepened it's time to
have fun.

Remember the hierarchy. Don't go straight
for hallucinations start simple and work
up to that well if you like.

Start with something like catalepsy the
looseness or rigidness of a muscle or
group of muscles. Use a visualization
technique.

"As you relax there going deeper focusing
on my voice listening to every word.

Anything I say will instantly and
automatically become your reality.

A FORCE 4 CHANGE

In a moment I'm going to ask you to open
your eyes, when I do your feet will be
planted in to the floor rooted to the
floor.

So much so that you can't move your feet.

Your feet are rooted to the floor like
two tree trunks. Solid you can't move
them. You cannot move your feet. You
perfectly safe and perfectly fine.

You just can't move your feet.

3.2.1. now open your eyes.

And your feet are rooted.

Now try and move them and see that you
can't.

Try really try. Try and step forward.

Now stop trying and ... SLEEP go deeper
and deeper."

Remember each time you get the subject to
open their eyes and get them to close
their eyes putting them back into
hypnosis they will automatically go
deeper.

Next another easy suggestion. A feeling
of humor.

"when you open your eyes whenever you
hear the word hypnosis it will be the
funniest thing you have ever heard. The

word hypnosis will be the funniest word you've heard.

And each time you hear hypnosis it will get funnier and funnier and funnier.

The funnier it gets the harder you laugh the harder you laugh the funnier it gets.

3.2.1 open your eyes.

Feeling ok?

Enjoying Hypnosis?

Did you think hypnosis would feel this good?

It's a funny word hypnosis?

Hypnosis is relaxing but feels good and can be really funny.

Hypnosis the more you hear it the funnier it gets.

Hypnosis hypnosis hypnosis.

Now SLEEP. And go deeper and deeper. The word hypnosis is no longer funny.

And you are no longer stuck.

The next time you open your eyes first person you see will smell amazing. The first person you see will smell so good you just want to know what it is.

They smell so good you want to smell it

more and more. You can't help but smell them it's so good.

3.2.1. Open your eyes."

Now hopefully you are the first person they see. If needed you can prompt them with

"Do you like my aftershave. Nice isn't it."

You will generally find that they will cling to you trying to smell you.

Even though their eyes are open you can still give them suggestions.

Click your fingers and say "Now it's the most disgusting smell. The most disgusting sickening smell."

Watch them try and get away from you.

"Now sleep. I no longer smell bad. Intact I smell good again but you no longer want to sniff me."

Its good not to smell bad lol.

"as you relax going deeper deeper deeper. Relaxing every nerve muscle fiber.

Now when you open your eyes you will no longer remember you first name. it will be on the tip of your tongue but you just can't remember it you just can't say your first name. your first name is completely wiped from your mind.

You know you know it it's just won't come to mind.

3.2.1. open your eyes your first names completely gone.

Hi I'm trevor and you are?

You must know your name?

The harder you try and find it the more you forget.

Can you tell me your name?

What's your last name?

Ok that's a good start. What's your first name?

Now sleep relaxing every muscle nerve and fiber.

Your names back you can remember it as you always could.

Now when you hear me click my fingers, whenever I click my fingers." *click your fingers a couple of times as you say this*.

"I will become completely invisible. That's right when I click my fingers I will be completely invisible you will no longer see me I will completely disappear when I click my fingers. But when I stomp

131

my foot I will reappear again." **Stomp your foot**. "when I click my finger's, I become invisible and when I stomp my foot I reappear." remember click your fingers when you say it and stomp your foot as you say it.

Now have fun with them while you disappear and reappear before their very eyes. Because for them you are actually disappearing and reappearing.

You can pick up objects and make them float. Make them believe you're a ghost. But be careful. We don't want them to freak out completely.

Remember safety. Although hypnosis is safe. If they injure themselves running away from you, then that is on you.

Now if you have achieved invisibility we can go for positive hallucination.

"now sleep. Relaxing every muscle nerve and fiber. That's it going even deeper.

This time when you open your eyes I will have completely changed into your favorite celebrity. That's right I look like I sound like I act like your very favorite celebrity. 3.2.1. open your eyes.

A FORCE 4 CHANGE

Hi How you doing?

Good

I know you know who I am but for the benefit of the guys that don't know can you tell them please.

Thank you.

If you could ask me anything in the world what would you ask?

Good question." try and give a good answer.

"Well it has been lovely to meet you. But I've got to go.

Sleep.

Now I'm going to bring you out of hypnosis when I do everything will be back to normal. I will no longer be that celebrity you can remember your name. but you will remember nothing that has happened here. You won't remember being hypnotized it will be as if we just started and nothing happened. Until I shake your hand. You won't remember a thing until I shake your hand then you will remember everything. And feel fabulous.

5 every muscle becoming less and less relaxed

4 take I nice deep breath filling your
lungs with cool fresh air

3 feeling that rush of energy as you come
around.

2 standing up straight

1 open your eyes feeling great.

How you feeling?

Did you enjoy hypnosis?

What was your favorite part?

Really?

Ok well guess it didn't work

Well shake my hand and we'll call it a
day."

Now watch their face as they remember.

Now take what you learn here, practice
and have fun.

Chapter Twelve
Other Fun
Suggestions

Here are some ideas you can experiment with and have some fun with.

Onion to Apple

Give them an onion and make them think it's a big ripe sweet juicy apple.

"In a moment when you open your eyes I will hand you a fruit. A big ripe juicy apple. The fruit I hand you when you open your eyes is a big ripe juicy apple.

You can't resist biting into it. Its delicious. So tasty.

3...2...1 open your eyes here take this tasty apple."

Hand them the onion and watch them eat.

Statues

Turn them into a statue.

"When I click my fingers, you will turn in to a statue. You will freeze in whatever position you are in just like a statue. When I click my fingers, you will freeze solid like a statue."

You can adapt this to happen when the music stops for a game of musical statues.

I'm A Super Hero

Just like the celebrity suggestion you can make them think you re anyone. From a super hero to a zombie. Do it just the same way.

Naked

Make them see everyone naked when you click your fingers.

"in a moment I'm going to ask you to open your eyes. When I do, every time I click my fingers you will see everyone naked.

Then when I stomp my foot they will be fully clothed again.

When I click my fingers everyone's naked

and when I stomp my foot they are fully clothed.

3...2...1 Click fingers and have fun.

Dancing Fairies

Make them see fairies or pixies.

And make them dance just for them.

"In a moment when I ask you to open your eyes. You will see fairies and pixies in front of you.

The fairies and pixies are here just for you and they are dancing.

When you open your eyes you will see fairies dancing just for you and its beautiful.

3...2...1...Open your eyes

They are beautiful dancing.

Watch them they are here just for you.

Tell me what you see.

Trees are Talking

Make them believe the trees are talking to them.

A FORCE 4 CHANGE

"When you open your eye's, you will see that the trees are alive.

The Trees are talking just to you.

And you want to hear them.

3…2…1…open your eyes and listen.

What are they saying?

Do they want anything?"

You get the idea

Some other things you could try include

- Make them believe they are the best mathematician in the world.

- The best motivational speaker.

- Make them sing everything so they can only speak in song.

I'm sure you can add more to the list.

Have fun. Be safe.

Chapter Thirteen Things You Can Do To Prepare

If you follow the hypnotic cycle remembering the pretalk is the most important part then you will get hypnosis.

But is there anything we can get the client to do to prepare?

Yes, there is.

Some of what we ask the client to do is visualize and imagine. But what if the client say I haven't got a very good imagination.

Well that's fine we can work on that.

Exercise one.

Hold an apple in front of you and look at it. Look at the stalk look at the shade changes look at the imperfections.

Now close your eyes and try to picture the apple in front of you and describe it.

How close did you get?

Now do it again.

Hold the apple in front of you and look at all the details the stalk the shade change, the imperfections. Now close your eyes and imagine the apple still in front of you and describe it.

How close did you get this time?

Keep doing it until you see it clearly in your mind.

Then change the fruit.

Then work your way up to the whole fruit bowl. This helps strengthen your visualization and imagination. You will get much better results.

As well as working on the imagination. Some people just can't relax.

Especially around the eyes. Or that tension behind the eyes.

Exercise Two

Now find a place where you can sit back
and relax with your head supported.

Good now I want you to roll your eyelids
into the back of your head.

Roll them all the way up as if your
trying to look through the back of your
head and hold them there for 3 seconds
then relax.

Repeat this 5 times then relax your eyes
completely and feel the relaxation. The
heavy relaxation spread over your face.

Then talk your way through the muscle
groups from the top of your head through
the cheeks, jaw, shoulders, chest, arms,
thighs, legs, feet and toes.

Just talk your-self down relaxing each
muscle group of muscles as much as your
eyes.

Working on visualization and relaxation
will increase success. And giving the
client these exercises as well as some
self-hypnosis exercises between sessions
will make each session more powerful.

Lightning Source UK Ltd.
Milton Keynes UK
UKHW020657120721
387033UK00010B/592